Copyright © 2025 by Alicia Davis
All rights reserved. This book or any portion thereof
may not be reproduced or used in any manner whatsoever without the publisher's
express written permission except for the use of brief quotations in a book review.

Printed in the United States of America

First Edition, 2025

HARDBACK ISBN 979-8-3485-1705-2
PAPERBACK ISBN 979-8-3485-1702-1
EBOOK ISBN   979-8-3485-1703-8

Red Pen Edits and Consulting, LLC
www.**red**peneditsllc.com

Welcome to Candy Hearts & Confident Starts: Loving Yourself from the Inside Out!

This book is all about YOU— girls like you who are amazing, strong, and full of potential. Inside these pages, you'll find sweet affirmations that will make you feel powerful, confident, and full of self-love. These affirmations are like a candy jar filled with positivity for your mind and soul. At Kadyn's Kandies, we believe every girl is unique and deserves to feel loved, kind, and confident. This book is here to remind you of how incredible you are! Each day, you'll find a new affirmation to help you feel positive, brave, and ready to take on anything that comes your way.

Affirmations are positive thoughts that can help you believe in yourself and feel happy inside. When you say them out loud, you're telling yourself how amazing you are. These words will help you feel confident, be kind to others, and love yourself just the way you are. When you feel down, open this book, read these affirmations, and know that they are here to remind you of your awesomeness. You are a bright star with so much light to share with the world.

Whether you're in middle school, elementary school, or just growing up, Candy Hearts & Confident Starts is here to help you remember that you are enough, and you deserve all the love and kindness in the world, so grab a pencil or marker, find your favorite place, and let's start each day with a big smile and a heart full of confidence!

Let's get started,
one sweet affirmation at a time!

I deserve good things to happen to me.
I believe I deserve happiness, love, and success. I am ready for all the good things life has waiting for me!

I am a shining star, full of light, love, and endless possibilities.
No matter where I go, I carry my bright light with me. I know that I am special and full of potential, ready to shine wherever I am.

I am unique, and I celebrate everything that makes me different.

There's no one like me, and that's what makes me special! I embrace everything that makes me unique, from my talents to my personality.

I love myself just as I am because I am enough.
I don't need to change for anyone. I am beautiful, smart, kind, and brave, just as I am, and
I celebrate myself every day.

I am proud of my achievements, no matter how big or small.
No matter what I accomplish, I will celebrate. Every goal I achieve is good, and I am proud of everything I do!

I am fearfully and wonderfully made.

God created all of us for a reason. We are valuable, one of a kind, and made with love.

I am proud of where I come from and the amazing family that supports me.

My history and my family are full of love and strength, and I honor them by being the best version of myself.

Every Day, I Grow Stronger, Braver, and More Confident.

Each day, I get a little bit stronger and braver. I face new challenges with courage and keep learning from them. With every new experience, I become more confident and sure of myself!

My dreams are important, and I am capable of making them come true.

I have big dreams, and I believe I can reach them. I know that with hard work, determination, and self-belief, I can make anything happen.

I am more than enough, and I don't need to compare myself to anyone.
I am proud of who I am, and I know I don't need to look like anyone else to be amazing. I am enough just the way I am.

I trust my heart and mind to lead me in the right direction.
I listen to my inner voice, trust my feelings, and know that I can make good choices every day.

I am proud to be myself, and I show the world the real me.

There is no one else like me, and that's something I'll always be proud of. I'm not afraid to show the world who I truly am!

It's okay to feel my feelings, and I can express them in healthy ways.

I know it's okay to feel how I feel, whether I'm happy, sad, or mad. I give myself permission to express my feelings and ask for help when I need it.

I love my body, and I am grateful for all it does for me.

My body is amazing! It carries me through every day, and I treat it with respect. I am proud of who I am, inside and out.

I am smart, creative, and full of ideas.

I am always coming up with great ideas and solving problems in my own special way. My creativity is a gift, and I use it every day.

I am in control of how I feel.

I am the boss of my own emotions. When things don't go the way I want, I remember that I can control how I respond. I can choose to stay positive, calm, and focused, no matter what happens around me.

I forgive myself and learn from my mistakes.

Everyone makes mistakes, and that's okay! I choose to learn from them and grow, knowing that I am always getting better.

I choose happiness and positivity every single day.

Even when things feel hard, I remind myself that I have the power to turn my day around with a smile and positive thinking.

I believe I can achieve all my goals.

I am capable of accomplishing amazing things, and I believe in myself every step of the way. My success is waiting for me!

I am not afraid to speak up and be heard.
What I say matters! I will speak up for myself and others with confidence and kindness, knowing that my voice is powerful.

I trust the journey of my life and know that good things are ahead.
I trust that everything happens for a reason. My future is bright, and I am excited for what's to come.

I am not defined by what others think of me.
I get to decide who I am by what I believe in and what I dream about. What others think of me doesn't change my worth or who I am. I am in charge of my own story!

I treat myself with kindness and practice self-love every day.
I am gentle with myself and treat myself with the same love and care that I give to others. I deserve love, inside and out.

I surround myself with love, kindness, and people who support me.
I choose to spend time with people who lift me up and make me feel good about myself. I deserve to be surrounded by positive things.

I am proud of my heritage, my culture, and my history.
The stories and strength of my ancestors live inside me. I celebrate my culture and carry their legacy with pride.

I shine with confidence, beauty, and love wherever I go.
My presence makes the world brighter. I carry love, beauty, and positivity, and I share it with everyone around me.

I am a role model, inspiring others to be their best selves.
I know that my actions can help others to be kind, brave, and confident. I lead by example and always try to do my best.

KIND
BRAVE
CONFIDENT

Be Bold. Be Beautiful. Be You.

Always be yourself and have the courage to stand up for what feels right to you. Being beautiful isn't just about how you look on the outside; it's about showing your kindness, your heart, and your strength inside. Don't be afraid to let the real you shine, because you are amazing just the way you are!

My Identity is Beautiful, Strong, and Something to Be Proud Of.

I love everything about myself, my skin, my hair, my culture, and where I come from.

Everything that makes me who I am is special and something to celebrate. Being myself is a gift, and I am proud of who I am every day. I embrace all the things that make me unique with confidence and love!

I am beautifully made, and I will never let anything dim my light.
I am a masterpiece, perfectly designed. Nothing or no one can take away my shine, because I was made to stand out and shine.

I am always learning, growing, and becoming a better version of myself.
Every day is a chance to grow. I love learning and know that I am becoming the best me.

Congratulations!

You did it! You've completed 31 days of building your confidence, kindness, and self-love. By reading and saying these positive words every day, you've planted seeds of courage and strength inside your heart.

Remember, the power to feel good about yourself and be kind to others is always within you. Every time you need a little boost or a reminder of how amazing you are, you can come back to these positive thoughts anytime. You are strong, smart, and worthy of all the love and happiness the world has to offer.

Keep spreading kindness, be brave, and always believe in yourself. You are a shining star, and nothing is impossible when you love yourself from the inside out.

Thank you for letting Candy Hearts & Confident Starts be part of your journey. We hope you carry these sweet reminders with you as you grow into the incredible person you are meant to be!

Candy Hearts and Confident Starts

Coloring Pages

About The Author
Kadyn Gillie

Kadyn Gillie, the daughter of Kim Gillie and Alicia Davis, is a native of Barnwell, SC, and the CEO and founder of Kadyn's Kandies LLC, a thriving business she launched at the age of 6. What began as a candy company has since blossomed into a brand that includes children's toys, accessories, Kadyn's Kandy Tees, and stylish items for moms and dads. Kadyn's mission is to spread beauty, boldness, and kindness, one treat at a time one child at a time. She is dedicated to inspiring children to believe in their potential while embracing confidence, kindness, and creativity.

As a young entrepreneur, Kadyn continues to shine as a role model in her community and beyond, growing her brand while staying true to her mission. Looking toward the future, Kadyn dreams of becoming an illustrator, combining her creativity with her entrepreneurial spirit. Whether through her business or her art, Kadyn is committed to uplifting others, fostering a sense of possibility, and creating a world filled with smiles and empowerment.

www.ingramcontent.com/pod-product-compliance
Lightning Source LLC
LaVergne TN
LVHW071659060526
838201LV00037B/380